A TRUE BOOK™

Pandemics

W9-CHS-683

KEVIN CUNNINGHAM

Children's Press®
An Imprint of Scholastic Inc.
New York   Toronto   London   Auckland   Sydney
Mexico City   New Delhi   Hong Kong
Danbury, Connecticut

Content Consultant
Elinor Accampo, PhD
Professor of History
University of Southern California

Library of Congress Cataloging-in-Publication Data
Cunningham, Kevin, 1966–
  Pandemics / Kevin Cunningham.
    p. cm.—(A true book)
  Includes bibliographical references and index.
  ISBN-13: 978-0-531-25423-3 (lib. bdg.)   ISBN-13: 978-0-531-26628-1 (pbk.)
  ISBN-10: 0-531-25423-2 (lib. bdg.)   ISBN-10: 0-531-26628-1 (pbk.)
  1. Epidemics—Juvenile literature. 2. Communicable diseases—Juvenile
literature. I. Title. II. Series.
  RA653.5.C86 2012
  614.4—dc22   2011007507

All rights reserved. Published in 2012 by Children's Press, an imprint of Scholastic Inc.
Printed in China 62
SCHOLASTIC, CHILDREN'S PRESS, A TRUE BOOK, and associated logos are trademarks and/or registered trademarks of Scholastic Inc.
2 3 4 5 6 7 8 9 10 R 21 20 19 18 17 16 15 14 13

Find the Truth!

Everything you are about to read is true *except* for one of the sentences on this page.

Which one is **TRUE**?

T or F Animal viruses never cause disease in humans.

T or F HIV can take years to show up as AIDS.

Find the answers in this book.

Contents

THE BIG TRUTH!

Two Sides of Technology

4

Poster with flu warnings

INFLUENZA
FREQUENTLY COMPLICATED WITH
PNEUMONIA
IS PREVALENT AT THIS TIME THROUGHOUT AMERICA.
THIS THEATRE IS CO-OPERATING WITH THE DEPARTMENT OF HEALTH.
YOU MUST DO THE SAME
IF YOU HAVE A COLD AND ARE COUGHING AND
SNEEZING, DO NOT ENTER THIS THEATRE
GO HOME AND GO TO BED UNTIL YOU ARE WELL
Coughing, Sneezing or Spitting Will Not Be
Permitted In The Theatre. In case you
must cough or Sneeze, do so in your own hand-
kerchief, and if the Coughing or Sneezing
Persists Leave The Theatre At Once.
This Theatre has agreed to cooperate with
the Department Of Health in disseminating
the truth about Influenza, and thus serve
a great educational purpose.
**HELP US TO KEEP CHICAGO THE
HEALTHIEST CITY IN THE WORLD**
JOHN DILL ROBERTSON
COMMISSIONER OF HEALTH

In 2009, the United
Nations estimated 16
million children had been
orphaned by AIDS.

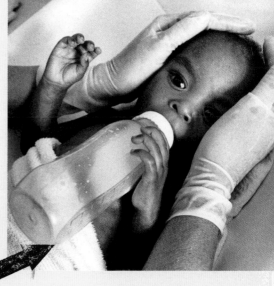

Explorer Christopher Columbus arrived in the Americas in 1492.

Smallpox: Pandemic Conquest

The term *pandemic* comes from Greek words meaning "all people." It usually refers to an infectious **disease** that spreads across a wide geographic area. A true pandemic is a disease that affects people all around the world. Pandemics could not take place before 1492. Up to that time, North and South America did not have contact with the rest of the world. Then the Spanish arrived with smallpox.

← Columbus arrived in America while looking for a new route to Asia.

7

Deadly Virus

The smallpox virus causes victims to break out in red bumps all over the body. Deadly and very **contagious**, it was a common childhood illness in Europe and Asia. The children who got smallpox and survived were **immune** to the virus for the rest of their lives. The native peoples of the Americas had never encountered smallpox. Native Americans were defenseless when the Spanish brought the disease to the Americas in the early 1500s.

Some historians believe European diseases eventually killed 90 to 95 percent of the native people in North America.

The Mexica believed Cortés was either a messenger from their god Quetzalcoatl or Quetzalcoatl himself.

At first, Hernán Cortés was friendly to the Aztecs.

Smallpox Enters the Americas

Spanish records suggest that smallpox killed one-third of the natives on the island of Hispaniola before spreading to other islands. In 1519, the Spanish nobleman Hernán Cortés landed in present-day Mexico. He set out to conquer the powerful Mexica (Aztecs). One of his generals brought someone infected with smallpox to the Mexicas' kingdom in April 1520.

Thousands of natives joined Cortés and helped him fight against their Aztec enemies and conquer Mexico.

The "Great Pox," as the Spaniards called the disease, raced through Tenochtitlán, the capital city and the largest city in the Americas. Thousands died. Mexica fleeing their homes spread the disease to other parts of the empire. The disease wiped out the Mexica army. Cortés easily conquered Tenochtitlán. Cortés became ruler of Mexico in August 1521. Smallpox continued to rage through Central America and beyond.

The Inca

The Inca Empire stretched from present-day Colombia to Chile. A smallpox **epidemic** spread throughout the empire in 1524 or 1525. It killed between 60 and 90 percent of the native population over the next few years. The emperor and most of his family also died. A war between two surviving sons to claim the throne further killed countless more. Francisco Pizarro, another Spanish conqueror, arrived in the 1530s and defeated the weakened Inca with fewer than 200 men.

Pizarro founded the city of Lima in present-day Peru.

Francisco Pizarro captured the new Incan emperor soon after arriving in South America.

Before the Pilgrims

When the Pilgrims arrived in New England in 1620, they discovered an abandoned Native American village called Patuxet. It became the base of their new settlement, Plymouth. Patuxet and the surrounding land were unoccupied because other Europeans had brought smallpox earlier. The disease wiped out up to 90 percent of the local Wampanoag people. It destroyed native communities from Maine to Cape Cod in the Massachusetts Colony.

Plymouth was the first European colony in the area we now call New England.

A vaccine helped wipe out smallpox in the 20th century.

Smallpox destroyed entire native villages.

The Great Pox

Smallpox left New England wide open to settlement by Europeans. Further epidemics in North America weakened native peoples for more than 200 years. Smallpox **devastated** the Pacific Northwest and, again, New England in the 1770s. It struck the Great Plains 60 years later. Historians believe that smallpox reduced some native populations so much that they could not protect themselves from European settlers.

Hindus believe that their lives aren't complete unless they bathe in the Ganges River at least once in their lifetime.

CHAPTER 2

Cholera: In the Water

Cholera results when the **bacteria** *Vibrio cholerae* infects a human's small intestine. **Dehydration** from diarrhea and vomiting may kill the victim unless he or she receives medical treatment. Cholera spreads in human waste and in water polluted by waste. Researchers believe the bacterium has lived in and around the Ganges River in India since ancient times. It wasn't until the 1800s that cholera became a pandemic disease.

⬅ Some of the most important Hindu festivals are held along the Ganges River.

Seven cholera pandemics have occurred since 1817. The deadliest began in the Ganges River region in 1852. Humans sailing aboard ships carried it around the world. Poor **sanitation** in 19th-century cities aided its spread by providing the bacterium a place to flourish. One million people in Russia died in 1854. More than 200,000 people died in both Spain and Brazil. In 1854, the same pandemic reached Chicago, Illinois, in the United States and may have killed 3,500 people.

In Russia, people mourned cholera victims in public ceremonies.

John Snow's Investigation

Cholera arrived in London, England, the world's most populated city in 1853. Medical experts at the time believed cholera spread through the air. Physician John Snow, however, thought people took the bacteria into their bodies by drinking infected water. An outbreak in London's Soho district gave him a chance to test his theory. He interviewed Soho residents and marked each case of cholera on a map.

Snow was also one of the first physicians to study anesthesia, the drugs and gases that allow patients to have pain-free surgery.

John Snow contributed a great deal to modern medical knowledge.

There have been seven cholera pandemics recorded throughout history.

Poor sanitation in London's streets contributed to the cholera outbreak.

Snow's map showed that cases of cholera were clustered around a neighborhood water pump. Water, he said, was the source of the disease. Human waste infected with cholera had leaked into the well from a nearby pit. Authorities removed the handle from the pump to keep people from using it. Snow's discovery helped reduce future **outbreaks**. After 1900, cholera appeared mostly in places with poor water treatment.

Struggling Against Cholera Today

On January 12, 2010, a major earthquake struck the Caribbean nation of Haiti. Millions of Haitians lacked access to clean drinking water or waste disposal. In October 2010, cholera broke out. Overcrowding and the earthquake's destruction helped the disease spread rapidly. The United Nations World Health Organization (WHO) responded, sending thousands of medical professionals and huge amounts of medicine. Their efforts were not enough to control the disease's spread. In five months, 3,600 people died.

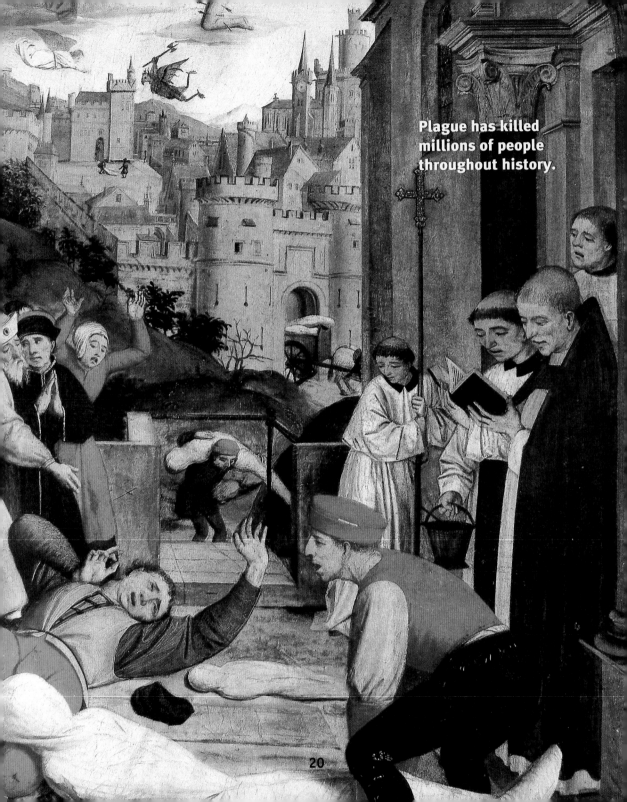

Plague has killed millions of people throughout history.

CHAPTER 3

Plague: Worldwide Killer

Plague is usually a disease that affects rodents such as rats and mice. But it can spread to humans. Bubonic plague occurs when a flea infected by a rat bites someone. This injects bacteria into the victim's body. Glands in the victim's armpits and groin swell. They become hard and sometimes turn black. The deadlier pneumonic plague strikes the lungs. It spreads from person to person when someone inhales water droplets coughed or sneezed out by someone already infected.

← The first recorded plague outbreak occurred in the sixth century.

As with many pandemics, the third plague pandemic was caused in part by poor sanitation.

There have only been three plague pandemics.

Plague in Hong Kong

Plague pandemics last for decades. The "Third Pandemic" began in western China in 1855. The disease spread slowly and reached Russia's Caspian Sea area in 1877. It moved from the interior of Asia to the coast and struck Hong Kong in 1894. Overcrowded conditions among the poor and a huge rat population caused an epidemic that killed 60,000 people in weeks.

Outbreak in India

Hong Kong, a British colony, was one of the world's busiest port cities. Rats and sailors carrying bubonic plague boarded ships steaming in all directions. British ships brought it to Mumbai, India, in September 1896. Tens of thousands of people fled the city and rapidly spread plague throughout the country. As many as 1,900 people died each week the first year. Twelve million Indians died before the pandemic burned out in the 1940s. No one is sure what caused the disease to disappear.

Health officials tried to isolate the ill. Many found this offensive.

Rats and Ships

Rats with plague scampered off a ship in Honolulu, Hawaii, in June 1899. The first victims were five people living in the city's Chinatown area. They died on December 11 and 12. Authorities tried to stop the outbreak by putting Chinatown under **quarantine**. The fire department burned buildings thought to have infected fleas or rats inside. A fire blazed out of control on January 20. More than 5,000 people lost their homes and belongings.

The burning of Chinatown added another element of tragedy to the plague pandemic.

Plague Enters the United States

Infected rats entered San Francisco, California, in 1899. California's governor, however, refused to believe the reports of plague that followed. Politicians, businessmen, and the Chinese community resisted an antiplague program until a new governor forced it on them. The outbreak killed 122 people. Infected fleas living on rats also spread plague to rodents throughout the American West. Prairie dogs, squirrels, and many other species remain infected today.

Each year, 10 to 15 plague cases occur in the United States.

Rodents, such as ground squirrels, are among the animal species that carry plague today.

Two Sides of Technology

Advanced medicine and knowledge about the cause and spread of diseases help the fight against pandemics. Yet, pandemics are still affecting millions of human beings. One reason is that poverty and the movement of large numbers of people still create conditions that allow disease to thrive. Surprisingly, modern technology and medicine have played a part in spreading disease.

Tuberculosis

Tuberculosis is caused by a species of bacteria that attacks the lungs. It infects about one out of three people worldwide. Only 10 percent of the infections, however, advance to active disease, where the victim suffers symptoms. In recent years, physicians have overused some of the drugs that treat tuberculosis. As a result, some drugs are no longer effective.

Malaria

Mosquitoes called anopheles carry a parasite that causes malaria. Malaria affects 225 million people each year. Years ago, a mosquito-killing chemical called DDT reduced or eliminated malaria cases in many parts of the world. But overuse of DDT made it less effective against all insects, including mosquitoes.

SARS

The 2002–2003 outbreak of SARS, a lung disease, killed 774 people and infected at least 8,000. Passengers traveling by airplane had spread the disease from China to the United States, Canada, the Philippines, and several other countries. Quick action by experienced disease fighters stopped SARS in a few months. On May 18, 2004, the WHO announced that the outbreak had been contained.

During flu outbreaks in the early 1900s, people were encouraged to gargle to avoid getting sick.

CHAPTER 4

Influenza: Spanish Flu

Influenza is a contagious virus found in humans, pigs, and birds. It begins as fever and sneezing and, in severe cases, worsens to attack the lungs. This causes a dangerous buildup of fluid, leading to a disease called **pneumonia**. Sometimes a virus undergoes a big change that alters its behavior. In 1918, a bird influenza virus may have mutated to infect humans. The disease eventually killed more people than any other pandemic in history.

 Influenza pandemics occur about once every 30 years.

INFLUENZA

FREQUENTLY COMPLICATED WITH

PNEUMONIA

IS PREVALENT AT THIS TIME THROUGHOUT AMERICA.

THIS THEATRE IS CO-OPERATING WITH THE DEPARTMENT OF HEALTH.

YOU MUST DO THE SAME

IF YOU HAVE A COLD AND ARE COUGHING AND SNEEZING. DO NOT ENTER THIS THEATRE

GO HOME AND GO TO BED UNTIL YOU ARE WELL

Coughing, Sneezing or Spitting Will Not Be Permitted In The Theatre. In case you must cough or Sneeze, do so in your own hand-kerchief. and if the Coughing or Sneezing Persists Leave The Theatre At Once.

This Theatre has agreed to co-operate with the Department Of Health in disseminating the truth about Influenza. and thus serve a great educational purpose.

HELP US TO KEEP CHICAGO THE HEALTHIEST CITY IN THE WORLD

JOHN DILL ROBERTSON

COMMISSIONER OF HEALTH

In the early 1900s, warnings helped to inform people about the flu.

Historians and medical researchers have long believed that the disease first struck U.S. soldiers training to fight in World War I. If true, the troops brought the disease to Europe. There it thrived in crowded, filthy, and wet conditions. Influenza hit the German army so hard that it had to cancel its knockout attack against France. The disease is called Spanish flu because newspapers in Spain were the first to report it.

Second Wave

The first wave of the disease began in early 1918. It made people feel ill and killed weak and elderly people. The second wave arrived after mid-1918. It was a killer of younger, healthier people. At Camp Devens, north of Boston, Massachusetts, more than 12,000 cases occurred in only 15 days. Special trains took away boxcars full of bodies that were stacked like boxes. Troop ships bound for Europe tossed dead soldiers overboard. In Europe, trucks followed marching soldiers to pick up those too sick to go on.

Hospitals overflowed with flu patients during the 1918 pandemic.

In 1918, U.S. Navy patients spent more than 1 million sick days in navy hospitals.

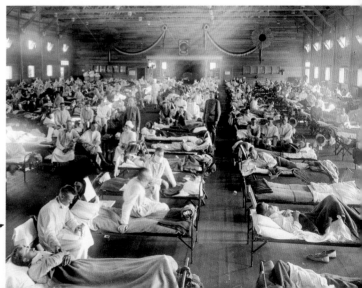

Many people wore gauze face masks to protect themselves from flu germs.

The virus caused nosebleeds and deadly fever. It choked victims by filling their lungs with fluid. Some suffered for days. Others left for work feeling fine but were dead by day's end. The medical system was unable to keep up with the growing number of victims. Hospitals in Philadelphia, Pennsylvania, turned away patients because they had no place to put them. The city ran out of caskets because so many people died.

Worldwide Disaster

Spanish flu entered India in Mumbai. It soon spread by people traveling on the country's railroads. At least 12.5 million Indians died. Millions more starved because there were too few people to harvest crops. On Samoa, an island in the South Pacific, 8,000 residents out of 35,000 died. Millions died in Russia. Spanish flu reached the last inhabited continent when it struck Australia in January 1919.

In Japan, 23 million people were affected by the flu.

Many in Japan wore face masks to avoid catching the flu.

During the Spanish flu's peak, almost no one went in public without a mask.

No one knows exactly how many people died of Spanish flu. In the 1940s, Australian scientist Frank Macfarlane Burnet claimed 50 million to 100 million people had lost their lives. Historians today usually say 50 million to 70 million died. At least 550,000 people in the United States died. Incredibly, the damage was done in just 18 months. Then, like all influenza viruses, Spanish flu mutated and vanished.

The 2009 H1N1 Outbreak

In early 2009, an outbreak of flu known as H1N1 began in Mexico. Soon, it had spread into parts of the United States, Europe, Asia, and elsewhere. It was declared a pandemic by both the United States Centers for Disease Control and Prevention (CDC) and the WHO. The two organizations tracked the disease as it spread around the world. H1N1 affected far fewer people than Spanish flu, with about 622,000 reported cases. Modern prevention and treatment helped to control the disease before it could turn into a massive pandemic. H1N1 killed fewer people than the average seasonal flu does each year.

Doctors around the world work to help patients with HIV or AIDS.

AIDS:
THE ONLY
"CURE"
WE KNOW
IS PREVENTION

CHAPTER 5

HIV/AIDS: Modern Pandemic

The human immunodeficiency virus, or HIV, attacks the immune system. It leaves the body increasingly defenseless against infections. Unlike smallpox or influenza, HIV often takes years to advance. A person with HIV may not know he or she is infected for nine to 11 years. The immune system has begun to fail by that time. At this stage, the condition is known as acquired immune deficiency syndrome, or AIDS.

 More than 25 million people have died from AIDS since 1981.

Mystery Disease

HIV probably first appeared in central Africa in the early 20th century. It remained unknown until the 1970s. A mysterious disease that destroyed immune systems surfaced in Port-au-Prince, Haiti. Meanwhile, physicians in California and New York noticed a small number of men with infections and weakened immune systems. An illness with the same symptoms had struck Tanzanian towns near Lake Victoria in Africa.

Timeline of Pandemic History

1853
Cholera hits London.

1520
Smallpox strikes the Mexica.

By 1982, U.S. investigators found that drug users who used needles had a great risk of catching the virus. It also infected others, including women and patients who received blood in the hospital. The CDC began tracking the outbreak. Researchers learned infected body fluids spread the disease. Experts named the condition AIDS. In 1983, separate scientific teams discovered HIV. Scientists believed a cure would be found.

1918
The Spanish flu begins.

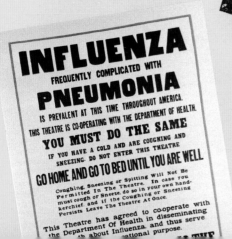

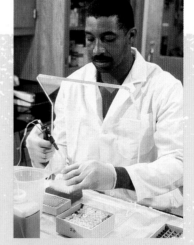

1983
Scientists discover HIV.

Catastrophe in Africa

But an HIV cure did not come. It took years to develop medicines to treat HIV. In the meantime, HIV spread quickly, especially in Africa. One reason for its spread was that public health officials often used dirty needles on their patients. A lack of information about the disease added to the problem. By 1996, 19.2 million Africans carried the virus. Five thousand more were infected every day.

Certain orphanages specialize in caring for children with HIV/AIDS.

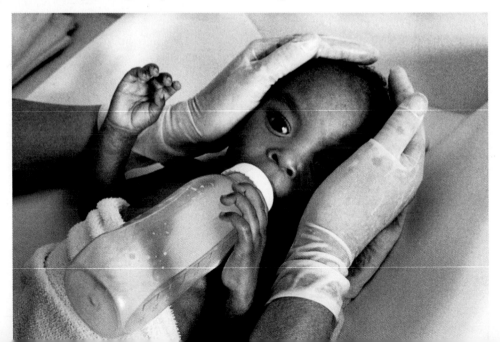

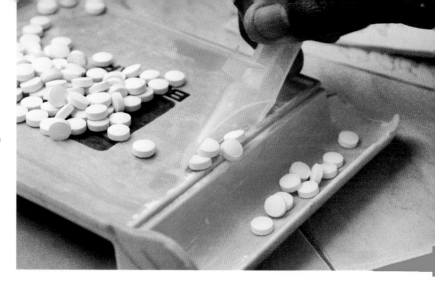

There is still no cure for HIV/AIDS, but medicine can help delay its effects.

About 70 percent of all HIV/AIDS patients are African.

New Groups at Risk

In the 2000s, HIV/AIDS spread rapidly in Caribbean countries, especially the Bahamas and Haiti. In 2005, inmates at U.S. state and federal prisons became three times more likely than other Americans to be infected. The disease continues to spread in eastern Europe. Health organizations believe that more than one million Russians have HIV, with 80 percent of them under age 40.

The Threat Continues

Education about HIV from organizations such as the WHO and the CDC cut the worldwide infection rate in the early 21st century. New cases decreased by 25 percent in the hardest hit nations. In the 1990s, researchers discovered that combinations of two or three drugs could slow down (though not cure) HIV. **Activists** around the world fought to make the expensive medicines affordable for all victims of the virus. ★

People line up for treatment and testing at an AIDS clinic in Russia.

In 2010, scientists announced research on a vaccine that lowers a woman's risk of catching HIV by about 50 percent.

Year smallpox arrived in the Inca Empire: 1524 or 1525

Percentage of Wampanoag killed by smallpox in New England: Up to 90 percent

Number of Russians killed in 1854 cholera pandemic: 1 million

Time it took for cholera to break out in Haiti after 2010 earthquake: 9 months

Number of people made homeless by the burning of Honolulu's Chinatown: 5,000

Number of malaria cases per year: 225 million

Number of people in India killed by Spanish flu: At least 12.5 million

Number of years it may take for HIV to cause AIDS: 9 to 11

Number of Africans with HIV in 1996: 19.2 million

Did you find the truth?

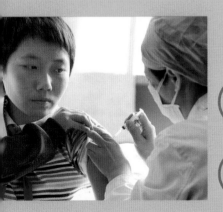

F Animal viruses never cause disease in humans.

T HIV can take years to show up as AIDS.

Resources

Books

Barnard, Bryn. *Outbreak: Plagues That Changed History*. New York: Crown, 2005.

Gedatus, Gustav M. *HIV and AIDS*. Mankato, MN: Capstone, 2000.

Green, Robert. *Pandemics*. Ann Arbor, MI: Cherry Lake, 2008.

Hoffmann, Gretchen. *The Flu*. New York: Benchmark, 2007.

Karner, Julie. *Plague and Pandemic Alert!* New York: Crabtree, 2005.

Krohn, Katherine. *The 1918 Flu Pandemic*. Mankato, MN: Capstone, 2008.

McPhee, Andrew T. *AIDS*. New York: Franklin Watts, 2000.

Ollhoff, Jim. *Smallpox*. Edina, MN: ABDO and Daughters, 2010.

Whiting, Jim. *Bubonic Plague*. Hockessin, DE: Mitchell Lane, 2005.

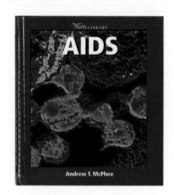

Organizations and Web Sites

CDC—2009 H1N1: Overview of a Pandemic

www.cdc.gov/h1n1flu/yearinreview/yir3.htm

Learn more about how the CDC dealt with the 2009 flu pandemic.

Frontline: The Age of AIDS

www.pbs.org/wgbh/pages/frontline/aids

Read interviews with AIDS experts and eyewitnesses, and watch a program on the history of the disease.

Places to Visit

The AIDS Memorial Quilt at the NAMES Project Foundation

204 14th Street NW
Atlanta, GA 30318-5304
(404) 688-5500
www.aidsquilt.org

Look at patches from the AIDS Quilt, a multiyear project to remember people who have died from the disease.

Wellcome Collection

183 Euston Road
London NW1 2BE
United Kingdom
+44 (0)20-7611-2222
www.wellcomecollection.org

See artifacts on plague, cholera, and malaria at this science and medicine museum.

Important Words

activists (AK-ti-vists)—people who work for change

bacteria (bak-TEER-ee-uh)—microscopic organisms

contagious (kuhn-TAY-juhs)—capable of being passed from person to person

dehydration (dee-HYE-dray-shuhn)—losing one's body fluids, especially water

devastated (DEV-uh-stay-ted)—very badly damaged or destroyed

disease (di-ZEEZ)—a sickness

epidemic (ep-i-DEM-ik)—an infectious disease that makes a large number of people sick at the same time

immune (i-MYOON)—protected from catching a disease

outbreaks (OUT-brakez)—sudden increases in the number of people with a disease in a certain place

parasite (PAR-uh-site)—an organism that lives off of other organisms

pneumonia (noo-MOHN-yuh)—a disease of the lungs

quarantine (KWOR-uh-teen)—a state of being isolated to prevent the spread of disease

sanitation (sa-neh-TA-shen)—the process of making things clean and healthy

Index

Page numbers in **bold** indicate illustrations

About the Author

Kevin Cunningham has written more than 40 books on disasters, the history of disease, Native Americans, and other topics. Cunningham lives near Chicago with his wife and young daughter.